All About...

Horses and Ponies

Fun facts and tips about your pets

Scholastic Children's Books,
Euston House, 24 Eversholt Street,
London NW1 1DB, UK

A division of Scholastic Ltd
London ~ New York ~ Toronto ~ Sydney ~ Auckland
Mexico City ~ New Delhi ~ Hong Kong

Editor: Sue McMillan

Published in the UK by Scholastic Ltd, 2014

Written by Anita Ganeri
© Scholastic Children's Books, 2014

ISBN 978 1407 12452 0

Printed and bound in Singapore by Tien Wah Press

2 4 6 8 10 9 7 5 3 1

All About...

Horses and Ponies

Fun facts and tips about your pets

SCHOLASTIC

Contents

Each year, thousands of unwanted horses and ponies are re-homed by the RSPCA.

This book has been created to help you to give your pet horse or pony a happy, healthy life. Read on and find out all about horses and ponies.

Quick quiz

How much do you know about horses and ponies? Take this true or false quiz to test your know-how. Then turn the page and read on to find out more about these amazing animals and discover if you've got what it takes to be a responsible owner.

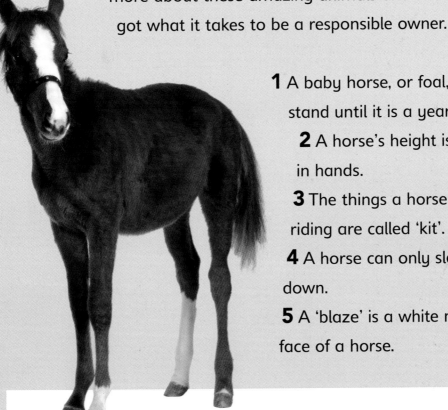

1 A baby horse, or foal, cannot stand until it is a year old.

2 A horse's height is measured in hands.

3 The things a horse wears for riding are called 'kit'.

4 A horse can only sleep lying down.

5 A 'blaze' is a white mark on the face of a horse.

Answers

1 False. For more about foals, see page 19. **2** True. **3** False. For more on riding equipment, see pages 74 to 77. **4** False. For more on sleep, see page 59. **5** True.

Meet the horse family

Horses are strong, athletic animals with hooves and swishing tails. Their bodies are built for running away from predators in the wild. The horse's super speed and strength has been useful for humans, too. For centuries, humans have kept horses for working, riding, sport and as pets.

Did you know?

In the Chinese horoscope, people born in the
Year of the Horse are said to be intelligent,
outgoing and energetic.

Four hoof-tastic horse facts

Eohippus   Mesohippus   Pliohippus   Equus

4 The first horse-like creature was about the size of a hare and had toes on its feet, instead of hooves. It was called Eohippus, and lived around 55 million years ago.

3 The next horse along was Mesohippus around 37 million years ago. This horse ancestor was sheep-sized, and browsed on leaves and shrubs.

2 The first horse with hooves was Pliohippus around 12 million years ago. Its whole body looked more horsey, with a sticky-up mane and long legs.

1 Equus appeared around four million years ago. Horses, zebras, asses, onagers and kiangs all belong to the equus group.

Horsey cousins

Horses belong to the same family of animals as wild asses and zebras. They've got loads in common with their cousins – they all run fast, graze on grass and like company. Time to meet the Equids...

African wild asses

African wild asses are the ancestors of donkeys – you can tell by looking at them. They're grey with stocky bodies, long ears and short manes. They're adapted for life in the deserts and mountains where they munch on thorny bushes and dry grass.

Asian wild asses

Asian wild asses look similar to their African cousins except they're bigger and have reddish coats, with dark stripes along their backs. There are two types – onagers from the Middle East and India, and kiangs from Tibet.

Zebras

Zebras live in Africa, mostly on the grassy plains. They're famous for their black-and-white stripes. Zebras are mostly social animals. They live in large herds and 'talk' to each other using braying and whinnying.

Six stripy zebra facts

6 No two zebras have the same stripes. Even the patterns on each side of a zebra's body aren't exactly the same.

5 If you see a zebra, chances are it'll be a plains zebra. They're the most common wild equids and make up two thirds of all zebras.

4 Quaggas were a kind of zebra that lived in the south of Africa. But bad luck if you're off quagga-spotting. Sadly, they were hunted to extinction in the late 1800s.

3 No one's quite sure what a zebra uses its stripes for. They may help it hide among the long grass or confuse a predator when it's faced with a big, stripy herd.

2 During migrations on the Serengeti, there can be up to 10,000 plains zebras in a herd.

1 According to African legend, the zebra used to be pure white until it had a fight with a baboon. The zebra tripped over a fire, and the fire sticks left dark marks on its coat.

Back to the wild

Przewalski's (per-zhuh-val-skee's) horses are wild horses from Mongolia. They're named after a Russian army officer who set off to find them in the 1880s. They're short and stocky, with thick, shaggy manes.

Herds of these hardy horses used to roam the deserts and plains. Then disaster struck. Their homes were taken over as farmland, and some were captured for riding. By the 1960s, there were no wild Przewalski's horses left – only a few remained in zoos all over the world.

The zoos worked together to breed the horses in captivity and, in 1992, 16 horses were released back into the wild. Today there are about 300 in special reserves in Mongolia and China.

Did you know?

In Mongolian legend, Przewalski's horses were ridden by the gods. The horses are called 'takhi' which means 'spirit' or 'sacred'.

Six facts about a horse's life

1 A horse can live for 25-30 years or even longer, if he's well looked after.

2 The best way to tell a horse's age is to look at their teeth. A young horse's teeth will be almost vertical. As horses get older, their front teeth grow longer and stick out. This is probably where the saying that someone is 'long in the tooth' comes from – it means he or she is old!

3 The oldest horse on record was Old Billy from Lancashire, England. When he died in 1822, he was an incredible 62 years old.

4 Horses are called different things, depending on their age.

Up to a year old: foal

Two to three years old: colt (male) or filly (female)

Four years and over: stallion (male) or mare (female)

5 A foal can stand and walk about an hour after he's born. A human baby can't do this until he's about a year old.

6 Thoroughbred horses have an official birthday. In the northern half of the world, it's on 1 January. In Australia and New Zealand, it's on 1 August.

Four pet horse facts

1 Horses and ponies are popular pets, with between 600,000 to one million in the UK.

2 It's thought that horses were first tamed about 6,500 years ago when hunters in the Ukraine kept them for their meat, skins and milk.

3 Horses can see almost right around them. They have two blind spots, one is directly in front of their nose and the other is directly behind them.

4 Although ponies are smaller than horses, some breeds have a thicker mane and tail.

Did you know?

Stuck for what to call your pet?
Take your pick from some of the most
popular horsey names:

1 Star
2 Blue
3 Magic
4 Beauty
5 Storm
6 Spirit
7 Splash
8 Dancer

Four horses of myth and legend

From ancient times, magical horses have galloped their way into people's myths and legends. Here are four of the most famous...

Pegasus

Myths: Ancient Greek

Appearance: White horse with wings

Supernatural powers: Able to fly vast distances. Carries the hero, Bellerophon, to kill the terrible Chimera monster.

Centaur

Myths: Ancient Greek

Appearance: Half-man, half-horse

Supernatural powers: Great healer and teacher of riding and archery. They teach many Greek heroes.

Unicorn

Myths: Medieval Europe

Appearance: White horse with a large, pointed horn on its forehead.

Supernatural powers: Legend says unicorn horn heals sickness and purifies water, making it safe to drink.

Sleipnir

Myths: Viking

Appearance: White, eight-legged horse

Supernatural powers: Able to gallop over land, sea or air. Carries the god, Odin, on many adventures.

Did you know?

One of the most famous horses in legend was actually made from wood. It was used to hide Greek soldiers during the Trojan War.

Horses of books, stage and screen

Horses have also played starring roles in books, plays and films...

War Horse

The hero of *War Horse*, a book by Michael Morpurgo, is a horse called Joey. He is bought by the Army to serve in World War I in France. His owner sets out on a dangerous journey to bring him safely home. The story is based on a real horse, called Warrior.

Sea Biscuit

Sea Biscuit is a film based on a US racehorse, Sea Biscuit. The horse is difficult to train, and his owner struggles to find a jockey. Eventually, he gives the job to Red Pollard. The two go on to win many races.

Secretariat

The film *Secretariat* is based on the true story of Penny Chenery, a housewife and mother who reluctantly agrees to take over her father's stables when he becomes ill. Penny works with a trainer and, against the odds, her horse Secretariat wins the US triple crown, coming first in three important horse races.

Black Beauty

Black Beauty is the star of a best-selling book, written by Anna Sewell in 1877. The story is told by Black Beauty himself, a handsome black horse. It tells of his carefree life as a young horse on a farm, to his hard days pulling a taxi cab in London, to his happy retirement.

Three horses from history

Incitatus

Incitatus was the favourite horse of the ancient Roman emperor, Caligula. His name meant 'speedy' or 'swift'. Legend says that Incitatus lived in a marble stable and wore a collar made from precious stones. He had his own servants to look after him. It is said that Caligula even considered making Incitatus a consul, the highest-ranked official in Rome.

Black Bess

Black Bess was the sturdy steed of English highwayman, Dick Turpin. In the 18th century, Turpin became famous for holding up coaches and robbing their passengers. Legend says he once rode faithful Black Bess all the way from London to York. Turpin was later arrested for stealing horses and hanged for his crimes.

Bucephalus

Bucephalus was Alexander the Great's horse and carried him into many battles. He was huge and black, with a white star on his forehead. A story tells how Alexander was the only person who could tame him. He did this by turning Bucephalus towards the sun so he couldn't see his own shadow which had been seriously spooking him.

Real-life horse tales

The horses in these three real-life tales needed their lucky horseshoes on. They became famous for surviving against terrible odds...

Christmas heroes

On Christmas day in 2010, when most people were sitting down to their lunch, a dramatic horse rescue was taking place in Shropshire. Ghillie, a mare, had fallen through ice into a deep lake. Luckily, she was spotted by a dog walker. The rescue team had to work for hours to chip away at the ice, as the water had frozen around her. When she was finally freed, Ghillie was warmed up and made an amazing recovery. Her rescuers were given awards by the RSPCA for their bravery.

The horses of McBride

In December 2008, snowmobilers in the Rocky Mountains in Canada spotted two abandoned horses trapped in the snow. They were starving and frostbitten. A small team of volunteers from the nearby town of McBride began a heroic rescue attempt. Using only shovels, they dug a 2,300 metre-long trench through the snow to reach the horses, Belle and Sundance, who both survived their ordeal, thanks to their rescuers. Their amazing story is now being turned into a film.

Trapped in the mud

In March 2012, a horse called Astro became stuck fast in mud in Australia. In a desperate race against the tide, his rider clung to him and kept his head up as he became more and more exhausted. After three terrifying hours, rescuers managed to pull Astro clear. Astro made a full recovery from the scary experience.

Horse power

For thousands of years, horses have worked on farms, down mines, and in cities and towns. Here are just some of the jobs hard-working horses have had to do.

Coach horse

Before engines were invented, horses transported people. They pulled carts, carriages, stagecoaches, fire engines, taxi cabs and buses. On long journeys, the coach drivers stopped overnight at roadside inns, complete with stables.

Farm horses

Before farmers had tractors, horses pulled ploughs and heavy machinery. Horses were also used to turn mill wheels to grind grain into flour for making bread. Horses have also worked in forestry, towing heavy logs.

Pit ponies

Pit ponies were used in mines to haul loads of coal. Many spent most of their lives underground, in cold, damp, dark conditions.

Did you know?

Concern over the welfare of working horses led to the creation of the RSPCA, or SPCA as it was then known, in 1824.

Search and rescue horses

One of the newest ways that working horses are used is in search and rescue. In some countries such as the United States, Canada and Australia, volunteer riders have searched for missing people. With horses they can cover bigger areas and they can also reach remote places.

Police horses

If you are out in a city, you may see police horses in action. These horses are specially trained to help police officers in many situations, such as for controlling large crowds of people.

Did you know?

'Horsepower' is the name of a unit of power. But one horsepower does not equal the power of one horse. In fact, a real horse is about ten times stronger than one horsepower.

Five warhorse facts

5 Horses have been used in war for more than 5,000 years. The first warhorses pulled chariots that carried soldiers into battle.

4 The earliest saddles were made from cloth and used by soldiers in around 700 BC. Later, leather saddles with stirrups made it easier for riders to stay on their horses and fight.

3 Japanese Samurai warriors fought on horseback. They were trained to use a bow and arrow without falling off.

2 In the Middle Ages, knights rode warhorses, called destriers. The horses had their own suits of armour, including a headpiece, called a shaffron.

1 Millions of horses were used in World War I. They carried soldiers, supplies, weapons, and messages. Some pulled ambulances. The RSPCA trained officers for the Army Veterinary Corps and also sent books and equipment to help the horses used on the front line.

Did you know?

The Animal War Memorial at Brook Gate in London was unveiled in 2004. It is a moving tribute to the millions of animals that died in World War I and World War II.

Three warhorse heroes

Here are just three of the many warhorses that have become famous because of the work they have done.

Black Jack

Black Jack was a jet-black army horse. His job was to follow the funeral processions of soldiers killed in action. He was not ridden but had a pair of boots pointing backwards in his stirrups to show the lost life. Black Jack also took part in four state funerals, including that of President John F. Kennedy in 1963. When he died in 1976, he was buried with full military honours.

Sefton

Sefton was a British army horse from 1967 to 1984. His nickname was 'Sharky' because he liked to bite. On 20 July 1982, Sefton was on his way to take part in the Changing of the Guard ceremony in London. A terrorist bomb exploded, killing four soldiers and seven horses. Sefton was seriously injured and had an emergency eight-hour operation. Despite being given little chance of surviving, this plucky horse made an amazing recovery.

Reckless

Reckless was a small but super-brave horse. In 1952, she became a pack horse for the US Marines in the Korean War. At the Battle of Outpost Vegas in 1953, Reckless made more than 50 trips across the battlefield, carrying rifles and injured soldiers, despite coming under heavy fire and being wounded twice. After the war, Reckless became a national hero and was promoted to the rank of Staff Sergeant.

Horses in sport

From ancient chariot races to showjumping, horses have been a part of sport for hundreds of years. Horse-racing is still very popular. Racehorses are sleek, fast and highly trained. Time to meet four of these sporting superstars...

Eclipse (1764-1789)

Eclipse was born in England during an eclipse of the Sun on 1 April 1764 and started racing at the age of five. From that day on he was never beaten, and he retired in 1770 mainly because no other horses were able to keep up with him. Today, Eclipse's skeleton is on display at the Royal Veterinary College near London.

Phar Lap (1926-1932)

Phar Lap's name means 'lightning' and he certainly lived up to it. Racing mainly in Australia, he won 37 out of 51 times races. In 1932, he travelled to Mexico to take part in a famous race. Despite the long journey and the heat, Phar Lap came from last place to first, winning the race in record time.

Secretariat (1970-1989)

In 1973, Secretariat became the first horse in 25 years to win all three top US races. And he did it in record-breaking time. Nicknamed 'Big Red' because he was large and chestnut-coloured, he was given many awards and honours for his amazing feat. This included being named as one of the hundred greatest North American athletes of the 20th century.

Frankel (2008-)

Frankel is a bay horse with a large white star, a white snip and four white feet. He is one of the greatest racehorses of all time. In his time racing, Frankel won all of his 14 races and more than £3 million pounds in prize money. During his last race in 2012, this horsey superstar was cheered home by a crowd of 32,000 fans.

Did you know?

The speediest racehorse on record is Winning Brew from the USA. In 2008, she ran at more than 70 km/h – as fast as a car.

More horsey sports

Playing Polo

Polo's a game played on horseback by two teams of four players. They hit the ball with long-handled mallets and try to score as many goals as possible in a 'chukka' (play lasting for 7.5 minutes). There are 4-6 chukkas in a polo match. Polo's incredibly fast and

furious, and polo ponies (they're actually horses) are built for stamina and speed. Players usually have more than one pony, so the ponies can have a breather.

Did you know?

Equestrian sports are very exciting but they can be dangerous for horses and riders. The RSPCA works with organizers of races such as the Grand National to improve safety and address welfare issues.

Eventing

Eventing is a real test of skill for both rider and horse. It takes place over two, three or four days.

- Trot-up

  A vet checks that the horses are healthy and fit enough to take part.

- Dressage

  The horse and rider perform a set of complicated movements that they've learned by heart.

- Cross-country

  Horses and riders follow a course across the countryside. There are fences, hedges and stretches of water for the horse to jump.

- Show-jumping

  Horses must jump over a set of fences or jumps in the right order. There are penalties for knocking fences down, or going over time.

Did you know?

At the London Olympics in 2012, Britain's Charlotte Dujardin won two gold medals for dressage on her horse, Valegro.

Built for speed

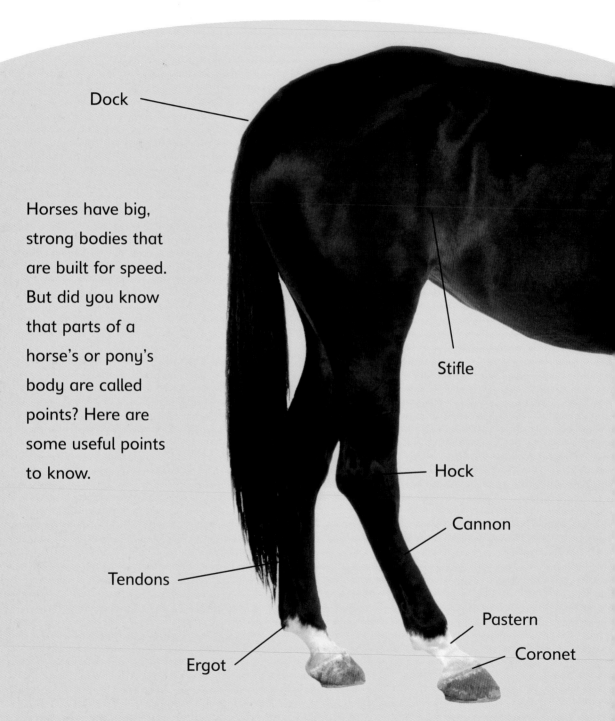

Dock

Horses have big, strong bodies that are built for speed. But did you know that parts of a horse's or pony's body are called points? Here are some useful points to know.

Stifle

Hock

Cannon

Tendons

Pastern

Coronet

Ergot

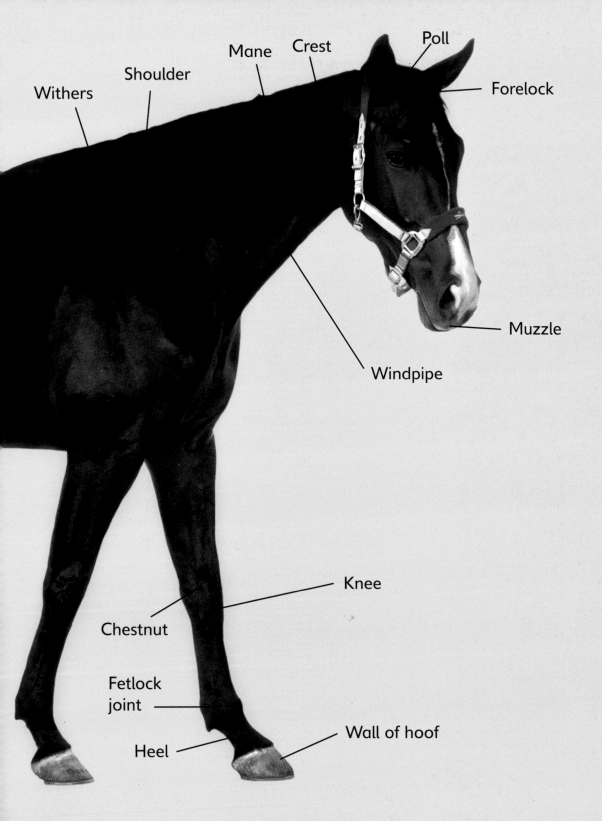

Withers

Shoulder

Mane

Crest

Poll

Forelock

Muzzle

Windpipe

Knee

Chestnut

Fetlock joint

Heel

Wall of hoof

43

Handy heights

A horse's height is measured from the top of its shoulders, its 'withers', to the ground. But don't bother getting your ruler out – a horse's height is measured in hands. Originally, a hand was the width of a person's hand but today, it's about 10 cm. So, a horse that's 16 hands high, or 16 hh, would be around 160 cm tall.

When is a horse a pony? When it's less than 14.2 hh – that's about 142 cm. Ponies are basically just small horses, and they make great first pets for budding horse owners.

Hand height (hh)

Did you know?

As well as a horse being the right size for you, look at his or her temperament and your riding experience. Do they match up? Will you be a good fit together?

Colour-coded

You can tell different horses apart by their different coat colours. But do you know what all the colours mean? Here's a quick spotter's guide...

Bay

Reddish-brown to dark-brown coat, with black mane, tail and points (legs).

Black

Black all over, including coat, mane, legs and tail.

Chestnut

Golden-brown coat; the mane and tail may be lighter or darker but never black.

Dun

Yellow-beige coat, with black mane and tail.

Grey

White or grey coat, gets lighter with age.

Palomino

Golden coat, with white mane and tail.

Piebald

Black and white
patches on coat.

Skewbald

White with patches of colour (not black).

Blue roan

Black or dark brown coat, mixed with white hairs.

Appaloosa

Coat with spotted pattern. Some all over, others have patches of spots.

Magic markings

You can also identify a horse by the markings on his or her face and legs. Here are a few to look out for:

Sock

White covers the fetlock and part of the cannon.

Stocking

White covers the leg, from the coronet to the hock or knee.

Snip
Small patch of white, close to the nose.

Star
White mark on the forehead.

Stripe
Narrow white mark down the face.

Blaze
Broad white mark down the face.

All kinds of horses

There are lots of different breeds of horses, with different sizes, looks and personalities. Each breed has different features, which tends to make them suitable for different jobs.

Four horsey types

1 Thoroughbreds are sleek, fast and graceful, with long legs and powerful bodies. They can run at speeds of more than 70 km/h, despite weighing around half a tonne. They are bred and trained for horse racing.

2 Arabians originally come from the deserts of the Middle East. The Bedouin people believed they were gifts from Allah and were so special they often shared their owners' tents. They're speedy and have great stamina and so many are used in endurance racing.

3 Lipizzaners are sturdy and athletic. They're also fast learners. At the Spanish Riding School in Vienna, Austria, they're trained to perform in spectacular shows. Lipizzaners are born dark brown or black, but turn grey, then white, as they get older.

4 Shire horses are huge and enormously strong. In the olden days they were used for pulling carts and wagons, and ploughing farmers' fields. Today, these gentle giants are mostly seen in shows and displays.

Did you know?

Horses can also be split into three groups, based on their blood types. Arabians and thoroughbreds are 'hotbloods'. Shires and heavy horses from Europe are 'coldbloods'. In between are 'warmbloods' – Lipizzaners and other sporty horses from Europe.

Four types of pony

Ponies may be smaller than horses but they also tend to be hardier. They often come from harsh habitats like moors and mountains, where being titchy but tough is useful for survival.

1 Connemaras come from Ireland. They're tough and can be good-natured. In the past they pulled carts, and carried heavy loads of rocks and turf. But today they are used for riding and jumping.

2 Welsh mountain ponies are hardy and sure-footed – handy skills to have in their rugged mountain homes. Like Connemaras, many Welsh mountain ponies are good at jumping.

3 Dartmoor ponies are one of the native horse breeds of Britain. They are small yet tough, with long manes and tails. They are often used for riding and jumping. Today, wild herds are still found on Dartmoor.

4 Shetland ponies come from the wild and windy Shetland Islands, off the northern coast of Scotland. The islanders used their tail hair to make fishing nets and lines. Shetlands may be small but they're also very strong.

Horse senses

In the wild, horses use their five senses to warn them of danger so they can run away. Horses and ponies that have owners to care for them still have seriously sharp senses and they are always on the alert.

Did you know?

Some people think horses have a sixth sense and notice things we don't. There are lots of stories of horses not wanting to ride past places that later turn out to be dangerous.

Hearing: horses have finely-tuned hearing. They can move each ear separately to pick up sounds from all around.

Sight: a horse's eyes are on the sides of his face so he can see almost all around him, even when he's grazing with his head down.

Smell: horses use smell to recognize others in their herd. To help them smell better, they sometimes lift their heads and curl back their top lips.

Touch: a horse is so sensitive that he can feel a single fly on his back and swish it away with his tail. Many horses also like being brushed.

Taste: in the wild, horses use their sense of taste to stop them eating poisonous plants. They like sweet and salty tastes, but not bitter ones.

Horsing around

Horses are sensitive creatures and can easily get lonely, scared or bored. To keep your horse healthy and happy, you need to make sure he or she has plenty of chances to spend time with horsey friends and be active.

Four tips for a happy horse

1 Horses are very lively animals. They must have a field or paddock where they can run around, and plenty of chance to use it.

2 Horses love company – in the wild they live in groups, called herds. You shouldn't keep a horse on its own – make sure he spends time with other horses he is familiar with.

3 Training your horse teaches him how to behave and makes him easier to handle and control. It takes time and you need to be patient, consistent and firm. Don't get angry or punish your horse. If you want to know more about training, ask an equine specialist for advice.

4 Take time to get to know your horse and how he behaves. If his behaviour changes, he might be unhappy or ill. Get advice from a vet or equine specialist.

Did you know?

Horses can sleep standing up. They lock the joints in their back legs to keep them upright.

Horse talk

Horses neigh and whinny, but they don't just use their voices to tell you how they're feeling. If you want to know if your horse is happy, sad or plain fed up, check out his or her body language. Here are some signs to look out for...

Calm horse

- Has a relaxed body
- Ears may be turned out to the side
- Head will sometimes be low
- Take care not to startle your horse. He or she may be dozing!

Interested horse
- Lifts head and looks alert
- Pricks ears forwards and eyes will look at whatever has caught his or her attention

Bored horse
- May chew the bars or wood of a fence or stable
- May weave from side-to-side in the stable
- May 'box walk' round and round his stable
- If you notice your horse doing showing any signs of boredom, contact your equine specialist for advice

Are you a top horse owner?

Owning a horse or pony can be brilliant fun, but you need to think very carefully before you decide to get a horse or pony of your own. Here are some questions to ask yourself if you're thinking of getting a horse or pony.

Did you know?

Owning a horse or pony is a big responsibility. If you own or look after one, you must care for them properly and meet all their needs to make sure they are happy and healthy – that's the law.

1 Have you had plenty of riding lessons and learned to look after a horse?

2 Can you afford to care for a horse?

3 Can you keep him or her happy and healthy?

4 Can you give him or her a good home and will they have the company of other horses?

5 Can you give him or her food and water everyday?

6 Can you make sure your horse gets plenty of exercise?

7 Can you call the vet if he or she gets ill?

8 Can you make sure your horse is looked after if you're away?

9 Can you give a horse the time and attention he or she needs?

Answers

To be a top horse owner, you need to answer **YES** to every question and many more besides. If you answered **NO** to any of them, think again about getting a horse as they are a long-term commitment and are expensive to keep.

Choosing a horse

How do you pick your perfect horse or pony? No two are the same. Think about your height, weight and riding skills. You need to match these to a horse's size, age and temperament. For example, if you're a beginner, an older, experienced horse or pony may be best.

Top tip

When you're going to look at a horse or pony, take someone who is knowledgeable with you. This could be your riding teacher or your vet. They'll be able to give you good advice.

Find out if the horse or pony you are looking at has any health or behaviour problems. Here's how to spot a healthy horse that has been well cared for:

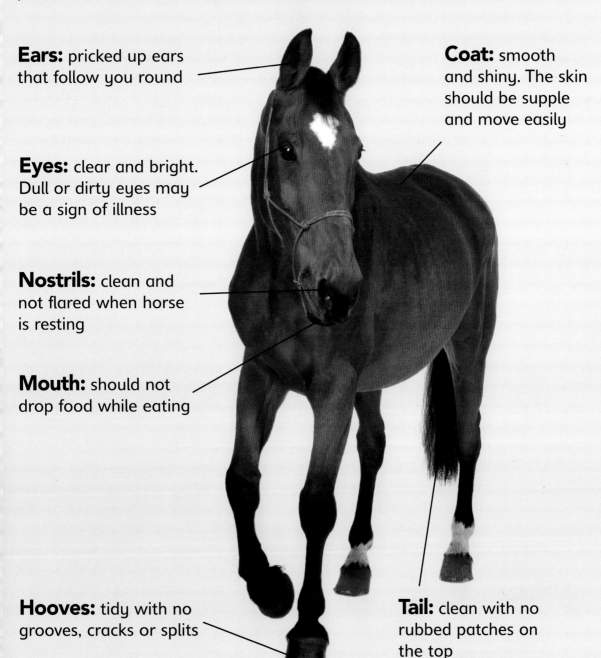

Ears: pricked up ears that follow you round

Eyes: clear and bright. Dull or dirty eyes may be a sign of illness

Nostrils: clean and not flared when horse is resting

Mouth: should not drop food while eating

Hooves: tidy with no grooves, cracks or splits

Coat: smooth and shiny. The skin should be supple and move easily

Tail: clean with no rubbed patches on the top

Living out

It is kinder and healthier for horses and ponies to live outside in a field for at least part of the day. Horses and ponies need time to be active and graze, but you still need to look after them. Here are seven tips about caring for your horse when he or she is outside.

1 Horses are sociable animals and need time to interact freely with other horses they are familiar with. Make sure the field's big enough for the number of horses. Each horse needs at least 0.5 hectare of grass to graze.

2 Check that your horse always has a trough of clean, fresh water to drink. In winter, you will need to make sure it doesn't freeze.

3 Your horse needs suitable shelter where he or she can get out of the sun, wind and rain. If you aren't sure how to provide this, ask your riding instructor for advice.

4 Fences and hedges must be kept in good condition. Make sure they are escape-proof and check for gaps and holes regularly.

5 Check the field every day for plants that are poisonous to horses. For more on poisonous plants, see page 71.

6 Check the field is safe, with nothing lying around that your horse could injure himself or herself on.

7 Check your horse over every day to make sure he or she is well and healthy, with no knocks, bumps or injuries.

Stablemates

If your horse is stabled, you will need to ensure that as well as a clean, well-ventilated stable, he also has access to a paddock where he can exercise and graze every day. A horse that's kept inside for too long can suffer, or become ill or bored. Here are some tips about stable care.

1 Make sure the stable's big enough and that it is clean and draught-free, with plenty of fresh air.

2 Stable partitions and doors should allow horses to see and interact with each other.

3 Fit a two-part stable door. Leave the top part open so that your horse can look out.

4 Put down plenty of good, dust-free bedding for your horse to lie on.

5 Your horse needs plenty of water to drink.

6 Try to do the same things at the same time every day – horses like to have routine.

7 Muck out the stable every day. Remove droppings or dirty bedding and make a clean bed for your horse or pony.

Did you know?

Let your horse out in the paddock every day so he or she can run around and do horsey things like grazing and spending time with other horses.

Dinner time

You must feed your horse a healthy diet to keep him or her in tip-top condition. Your horse should be given as much chance to graze as possible – unless your vet has advised you differently. Also make sure your horse or pony has free access to clean, fresh water.

Six top tips for feeding your horse

1 Horses need a regular supply of grass or hay (forage) so they can eat throughout the day.

2 Over winter, horses living out may also need extra hard feed (horse cubes or grain).

3 Put your horse's food trough on the ground – it's a more natural way for a horse to eat.

4 Grass clippings and large amounts of apples can be harmful to horses.

5 Don't let your horse get overweight. It can lead to painful hoof problems and is unhealthy.

6 If you change your horse's diet, do it slowly over about two weeks.

Did you know?

Some plants are deadly poisonous for horses. Here are a few to look out for in your field:

Ragwort

Foxgloves

Yew

Oak

Leyland Cypress

Riding out

Once you've got to know your horse or pony and he or she has settled in, it is time to practise what you have learned in your lessons. Let's put your horse through his paces, or gaits.

A. Walk

This is the slowest movement your horse makes. Its hooves make a '1-2-3-4' beat on the ground. Your horse puts one foot on the ground in turn, with one foot on the ground at all times.

B. Trot

The trot is quicker, with a '1-2, 1-2' beat. Your horse brings one back leg and the opposite front leg forward at the same time so he or she is moving their legs as diagonal pairs. Then they swing the other two legs forward.

C. Canter

A cantering horse bounces along the ground. The canter has a '1-2-3' beat – one back leg hits the ground, followed by a diagonal pair, then the front leg. Then he or she starts again.

D. Gallop

The gallop's even faster and this is for experienced riders only. It's like the canter but with a fast '1-2-3-4' beat, with the horse's four feet landing separately.

Did you know?

Having lessons from a good instructor will help you to be a good rider. It is also kinder and safer for your horse.

Riding kit

Before you go riding, it's very important to make sure the kit for both you and your horse fits properly and is comfortable. Here you can find out what you should both be wearing.

Your horse needs...

• A saddle – this fits on your horse's back for you to sit on. It helps you to sit in the correct position. It's often placed on a soft pad to stop it rubbing your horse's skin.

- A bridle – this fits over your horse's head and allows you to guide and control him. The bridle has a bit that goes in the horse's mouth. The reins attach to the bit and go over the horses's head for the rider to hold.

Top tip

Your horse's bits of kit are called tack. It's really important to look after your tack properly. After every ride, clean it and check it for wear and tear.

You need...

- A riding hat – this protects your head and is a must for safety. It must fit properly, follow current safety standards and have a chin strap. If you have a fall, get an adult to check your hat and replace it if necessary.

- Riding boots – these are the best and safest choice of footwear.

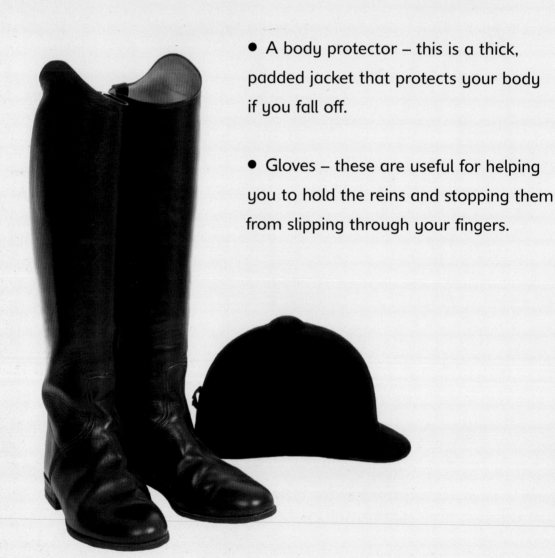

- A body protector – this is a thick, padded jacket that protects your body if you fall off.

- Gloves – these are useful for helping you to hold the reins and stopping them from slipping through your fingers.

Grooming

To keep your horse's coat looking sleek and shiny, you need to groom him or her regularly. In the wild, horses groom each other but pet horses need your help. First, you'll need a good grooming kit:

Sweat scraper
to remove excess water and sweat

Hoof oil and brush
for keeping hooves healthy

Body brush
for brushing off mud and dirt

Metal curry comb
for cleaning your body brush. This should not be used directly on your horse

Plastic curry comb
used to get rid of mud and dirt

Hoof pick
for cleaning hooves

Soft dandy brush
for removing oils and dust

Rubber curry comb
used in a circular motion to get rid of loose hair

Grooming rag
to give final polish to coat

Soft sponges
one for the eyes, nose and mouth, another for the dock

Mane comb
to remove tangles

Top tip

Grooming your horse or pony is important to get rid of any dirt in his or her coat, otherwise this could rub against the tack. Grooming is a great way of bonding with your horse, too!

Lucky horseshoes

If you ride your horse on hard ground, his or her feet get a lot of wear and tear. Looking after your horse's feet and hooves is an important part of a horse-owner's job.

Most riding horses and ponies are fitted with metal horseshoes. A farrier makes and fits these shoes by nailing them on to the horse's hooves. Don't worry – it doesn't hurt. The farrier also trims the hooves – it's like cutting your fingernails. Most horses need new shoes about every four to six weeks. Even if your horse does not wear shoes, his hooves should still be regularly checked by a farrier.

You should also pick out your horse's hooves with a hoof pick, see page 78. This means cleaning out any mud or stones. Do this every day, and before and after rides.

Did you know?

Some people believe hanging a horseshoe on the door will bring good luck. But only if the two ends are pointing upwards. If they point downwards, it's said to be unlucky.

Ask a vet

Part of being a good horse owner is making sure your pet's happy and healthy. Here are some questions you might want to ask your vet.

Q: I love horses and want to learn to ride. Where should I go?

A: A good way to learn is to take lessons at a riding school. Look for one that's approved by the British Horse Society or Association of British Riding Schools.

Q: What routine treatment does my horse need?

A: Horses should be vaccinated against tetanus and equine influenza. They should also be wormed regularly. Their teeth, which grow constantly, should also be checked at least annually by a vet or an equine dentist, to make sure there are no sharp edges on the back teeth, which could be painful.

Q: Does my horse need insurance?

A: If your horse or pony does fall ill, insurance can cover the cost of expensive treatment.

Q: How often does the vet need to see my horse?

A: When you are buying a horse or pony it is a good idea to get a vet to check him out beforehand. You may need to do this to get insurance. After this, he will need a check up at least once a year. If he looks ill, injured or he is in pain, or his eating habits or behaviour changes, call your vet immediately.

Q: What is the best way of taking my horse to a show?

A: Transport can be stressful for a horse or pony. Choose a horsebox or horse lorry that is the right size for your horse. Make sure it is driven carefully and don't travel too long without a break.

Common horse problems

Q: My horse is limping. What do I do?

A: Your horse may have a stone in their shoe. Stop riding him and pick his feet out. If he's still limping, he may have a more serious problem. Call the vet immediately.

Q: I fell off my horse last week and now I'm too scared to ride. What should I do?

A: Most riders fall off at some point but it can make you lose your confidence. Ask your instructor for advice and to try to get back on a horse as soon as you can.

Q: What's poisonous to horses?

A: As well as the plants mentioned on page 71 – ragwort, foxglove, yew, leyland cypress and oak – you must also make sure that your horse does not come into contact with plants treated with weed killer or rodent poisons. If you suspect your horse may have been poisoned, contact your vet immediately.

Q: My horse keeps pawing at the ground. What's wrong with her?

A: There is a chance she may have colic. Ask a knowledgeable adult for advice and if they feel it is necessary, call a vet at once.

Q: It's winter and my horse lives out. What should I do?

A: Horses grow thicker coats in winter but he or she may still need a rug to keep warm. Choose a rug that's waterproof with a warm lining. It should fit snugly and cover his or her sides.

Horses quiz

1. Which of these isn't a horsey cousin?
a) zebra
b) wild ass
c) hippopotamus

2. What special feature did Pegasus have?
a) wings
b) horn on nose
c) eight legs

3. What is a horse's height measured in?
a) feet
b) hands
c) heads

4. What colour is a piebald?

a) brown and white

b) black and white

c) grey

5. What does a farrier do?

a) Cares for horses' teeth

b) Cares for horses' hooves and fits horseshoes

c) Makes saddles and bridles

6. Which horse did Dick Turpin ride?

a) Black Jack

b) Black Beauty

c) Black Bess

7. What does it mean when a horse puts their ears forward?
a) they are interested
b) they are happy
c) they are frightened

8. Which of these plants is poisonous to horses?
a) ragwort
b) oak
c) yew

9. What do you use a dandy brush for?
a) brushing mud off the coat
b) combing the mane and tail
c) cleaning the feet

10 How long do most horses live?
a) 15-20 years
b) 25-30 years
c) 35-40 years

Answers

1. c) 2. a) 3. b) 4. b) 5. b) 6. c) 7. a) 8. a) b) c) 9. a) 10. b)

Horse trivia

1 A horse's eyes can work independently, so that he or she sees two different images at once!

2 Horses and ponies can only breathe through their noses.

3 Because a horse's teeth keep growing, grazing helps to grind the teeth down. Even so, your equine dentist or vet may need to file them down once a year.

4 Like humans, horses tend to have a dominant side. This is known as being left-lead or right-lead. It's a little like being left-handed or right-handed.

5 In a herd of wild horses, it is an older mare that leads the group.

6 A foal has 24 baby teeth.

7 Horses poo up to 14 times a day.

8 Most foals are born at night.

9 A horse sleeps for about three hours a day, taking several short naps.

10 The middle V-shaped part of a horse's hoof is called the 'frog'.

All about the RSPCA

The RSPCA, or Royal Society for the Prevention of Cruelty to Animals, was founded in 1824 in London. It was the first British animal welfare charity and was originally mostly concerned with the welfare of animals such as pit ponies that worked down in the coal mines. The charity also worked with the hundreds of thousands of animals that served in the military during the First and Second World Wars.

Since then, the RSPCA has worked tirelessly to improve the lives of millions of animals, including those kept as pets and farm animals. It has 170 branches around the country, where staff and volunteers care for the animals that come into the centres. Many are re-homed after they have been nursed back to health and enjoy happiness with their new owners.

By educating people about animal welfare, the RSPCA aims to make sure that all animals live healthy, happy lives and are treated with compassion and respect.

To find out more visit: **www.rspca.org.uk**

Index

Also available